EASY SCRIPT LETTERING WORKBOOK IS THE WORK OF LETTERING ARTIST CJ HUGHES. ALL PARTS OF THIS WORKBOOK, INCLUDING THE TEXT AND IMAGERY, ARE COPYRIGHT 2017 CJ HUGHES and may not be used without permission.

contact the author/artist at:
cj@cjhugheslettering.com

FOR EVEN MORE LETTERING WORKBOOKS VISIT:
CJHughesLettering.com

(C) 2017 CJ Hughes. All rights reserved. No duplication, resale or uploading permitted.

Easy Script Lettering Workbook
by CJ Hughes

While there are many books on the market concerning the intricacies of hand lettering, this beginner tutorial is meant to be as easy to understand and use as possible. There is a minimal amount of instruction, just the basics to get you started lettering right away. If you follow the simple guidelines and techniques found here you will be freehand lettering in no time. Each Easy Lettering workbook covers one distinct lettering style.

I recommend using Crayola broad tip markers for this Easy Lettering workbook.
They are easy to find and easy to use. Their tips have just the right amount of firmness and flexibility for thin to thick lettering. You can use Sharpie fine point markers as well, but they won't have as much flexibility at the nib as a Crayola marker. Once you have mastered the strokes in this workbook using markers you can move on to using the same techniques with paintbrush and ink or paintbrush and watercolors or acrylics. Brushes are harder to control which is why I recommend learning with markers.

If you don't wish to letter directly into the workbook you can purchase a tracing paper pad and lay a sheet over the page you want to work on.

The grayed out letters and practice shapes are meant to be drawn over. As you move across each line, the letter form becomes lighter. There is a blank space for you to draw the letter on your own at the end. Compare your last freehand letter with the example at the front of the line. If you still need practice, reprint and use that sheet until you are happy with your final freehand letter.

TIPS FOR GREAT LETTERING

Use a clear, flat workspace. If your table has texture, use the back of a drawing pad to get a smooth writing space.

Make sure there is no clutter around your workspace. You will need room to move your whole arm from the shoulder.

Use a sturdy chair - nothing with wheels.

Grip the marker firmly with your normal pencil or pen grip. Practice drawing a large C in the air while keeping your wrist, elbow and shoulder locked. Start at the top of the C and roll all of your fingers around and down towards your thumb. Now reverse this motion. These are the two basic motions you will use to draw script lettering.

Make an effort to keep your back straight. Try not to crouch over your work area or lean in too much. Keeping a more erect posture will allow your arm to move freely from the shoulder.

Down strokes are thick, upstrokes are thin. Cross strokes can be thin. thick, or a combination. There is an example page showing each of these methods. This is the most important thing to remember when lettering a thin/thick script alphabet.

Curve the tops and bottoms of your lowercase letters to make words easier to read. Sharp points at the tops and bottoms of letters make them difficult to read.

For more free form lettering, vary your baseline, the line the bottom of your letters rest on, or draw your words on arcs and curves . You will find examples of this in the book and can use the guidelines to practice writing your own words.

When drawing thick down strokes, the end of the marker should be at a slight angle to the paper. Allow most of the side of the marker point to make contact with the paper. When drawing the thin upstrokes, bring the pen tip up to where just the point is resting on the paper. This means that the marker will need to change position in your grip between then and thick lines. This will seem awkward at first but the switch will become more natural the more you practice. When you reach the end of a letter pull up and flick the pen slightly. Drawing each letter separately gives you more control over the final product. It also makes for cleaner lettering that is beautiful and easy to read.

Keep a fluid movement. Do not allow your pen to rest in one spot too long or you will get end dots.

Remember, the harder the pressure or the longer you take to draw a stroke, the thicker it will be. The opposite is also true.

Once you are ready to move on from the workbook and start crafting your own words and phrases there is a simple process to follow. On a sheet of paper, draw your guidelines with pencil. Draw a line for the top of the capital letters, the top of the lowercase letters, and then for the bottom of your letters. Remember, the top of your lower case letters guideline should be slightly above the middle point of your top and bottom guidelines. Next, write in your word or words with a pencil. Leave space between the letters to allow for the thick down strokes. Now, use your marker to write out your words over the pencil lines as you've been practicing; thick down strokes, thin upstrokes. When you are finished, erase your pencil guidelines. Once you have mastered these lettering techniques try what you've learned using a paintbrush with ink or paint. You can also experiment with other kinds of markers and pens.

Happy Lettering!

CJ Hughes
www.customchalk.com
www.cjhugheslettering.com
www.Instagram.com/cjhugheslettering

Aa Bb Cc Dd
Ee Ff Gg Hh
Ii Jj Kk Ll
Mm Nn Oo Pp
Qq Rr Ss Tt
Uu Vv Ww Xx

Yy Zz

12345
67890
& & ?!
# @ $ ~

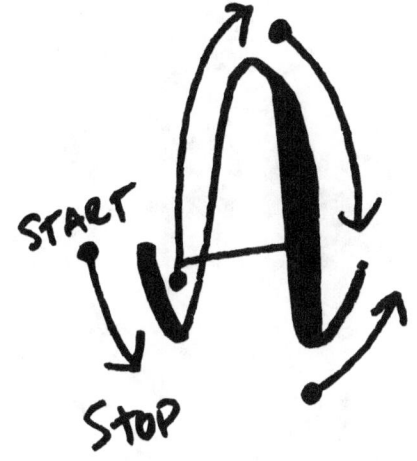

In the beginning pick up the marker point after each stroke.

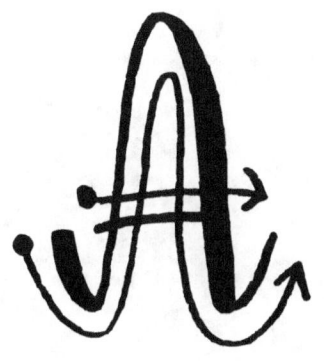

As you get more comfortable, you can treat each letter as one movement - completing all of the thin and thick strokes in just one or two movements per letter.

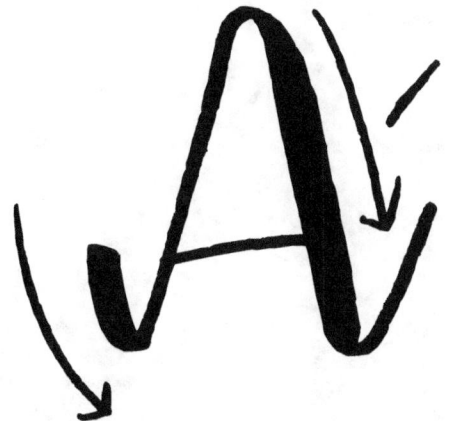

Downstrokes
Angle the marker tip slightly so that more of the edge touches the Paper. Press down firmly.

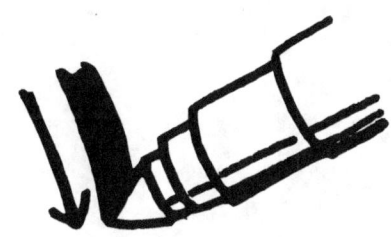

UPSTROKES
Hold the marker at ABOUT 90 DEGREES from the paper and apply light pressure through the stroke.
Use only the point of the marker.

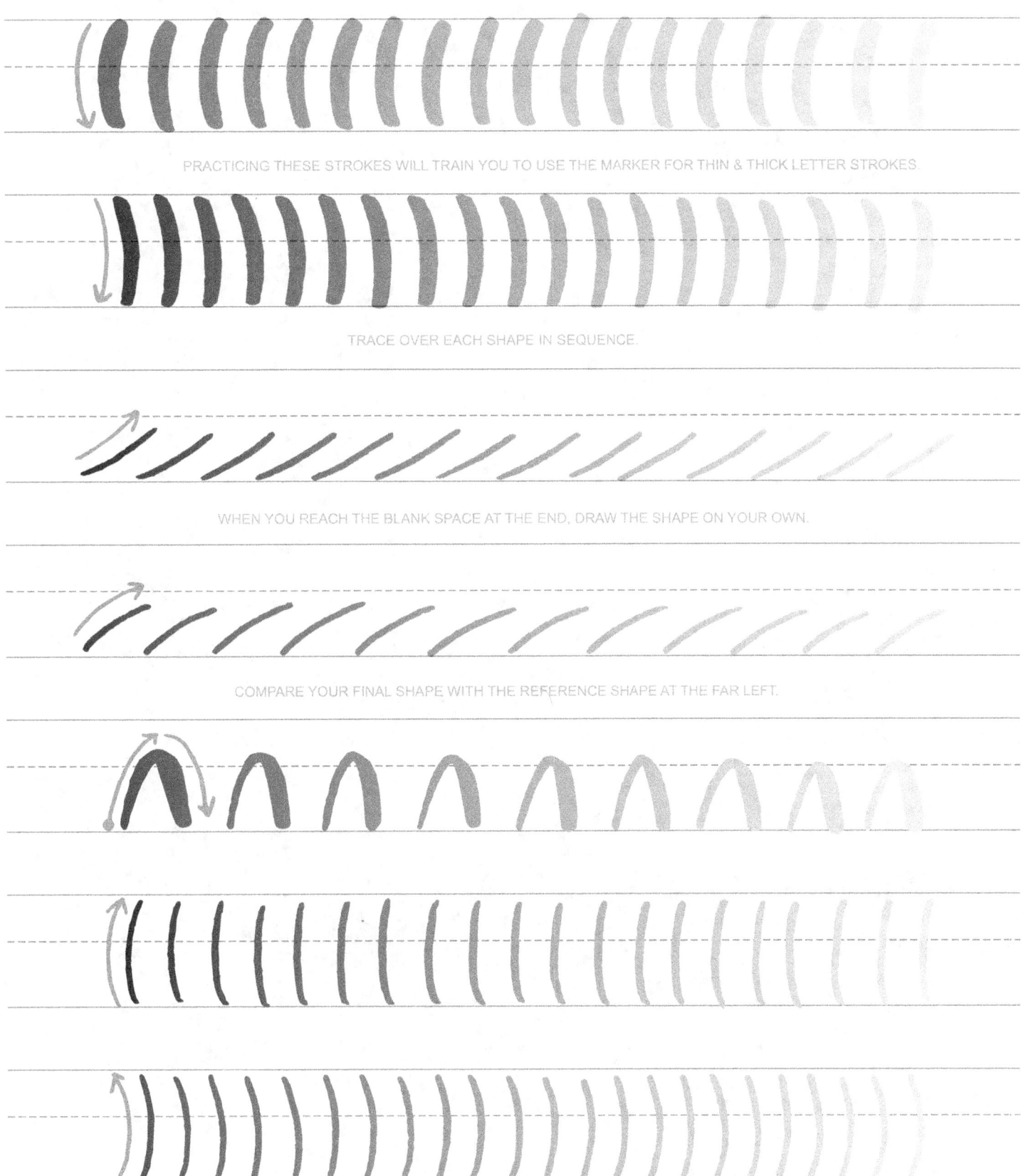

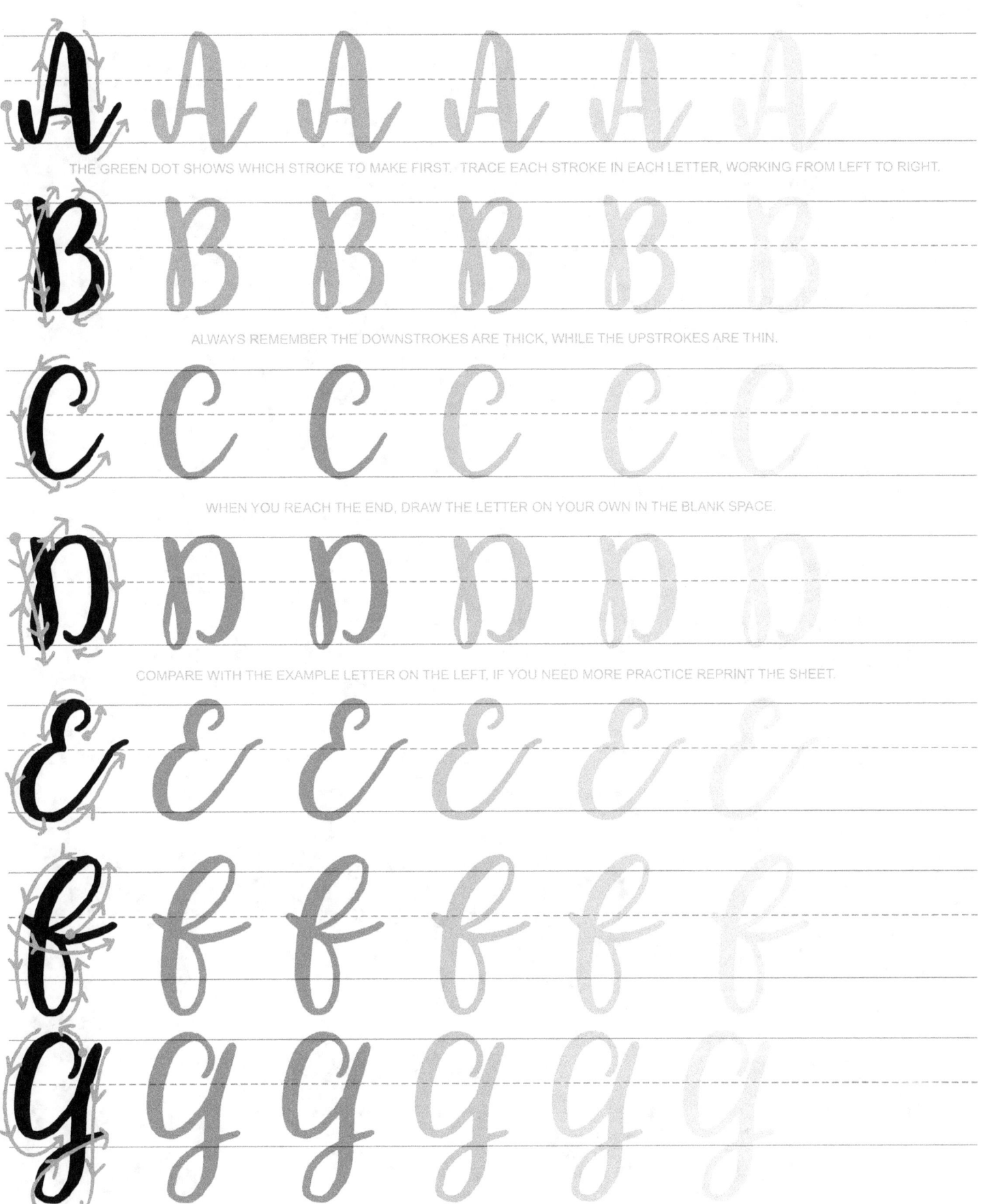

H H H H H

d d d d d

J J J J J

K K K K K

L L L L L

m m m m m

n n n n n

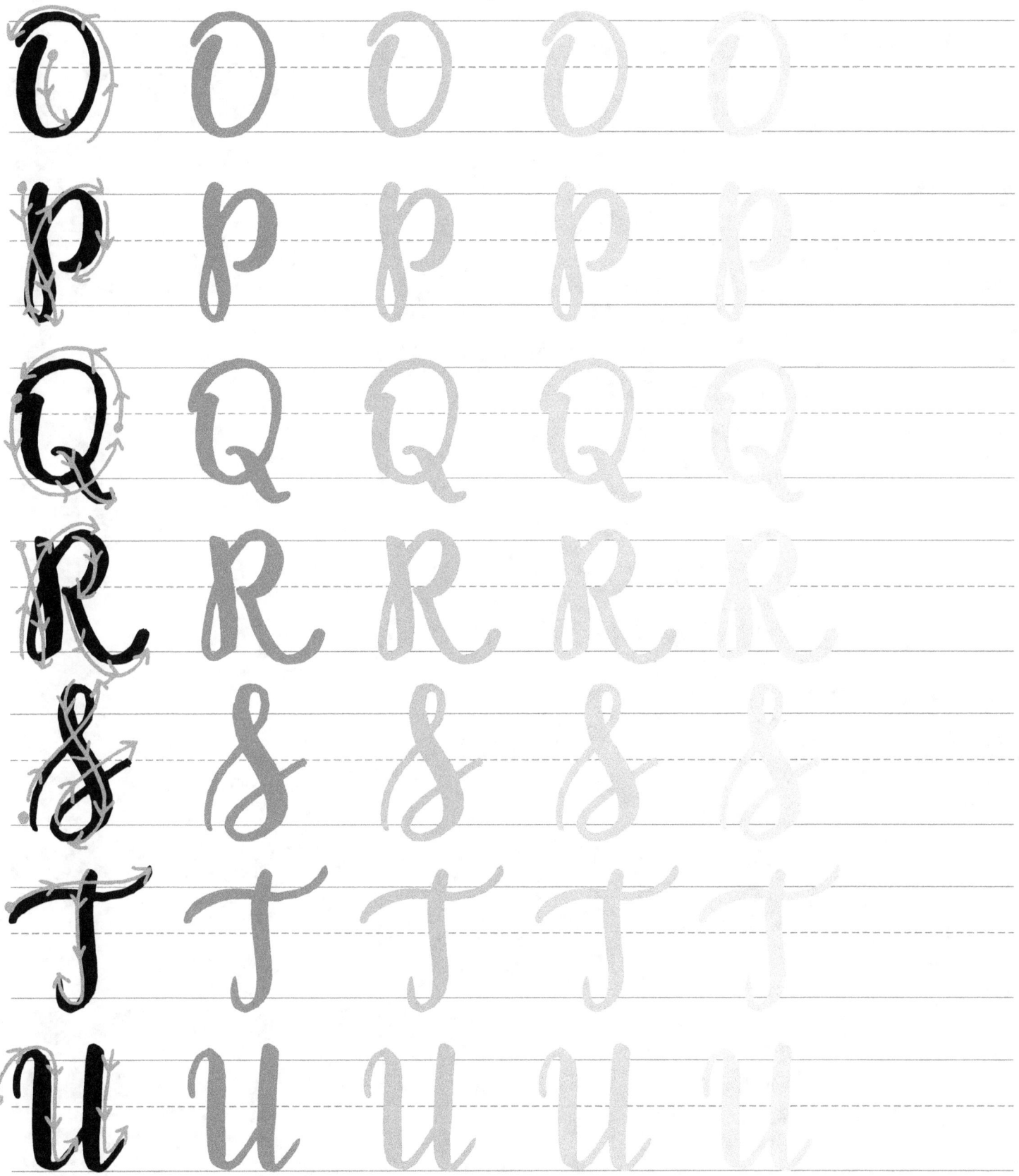

V V V V V
W W W W W
X X X X X
Y Y Y Y Y
Z Z Z Z Z

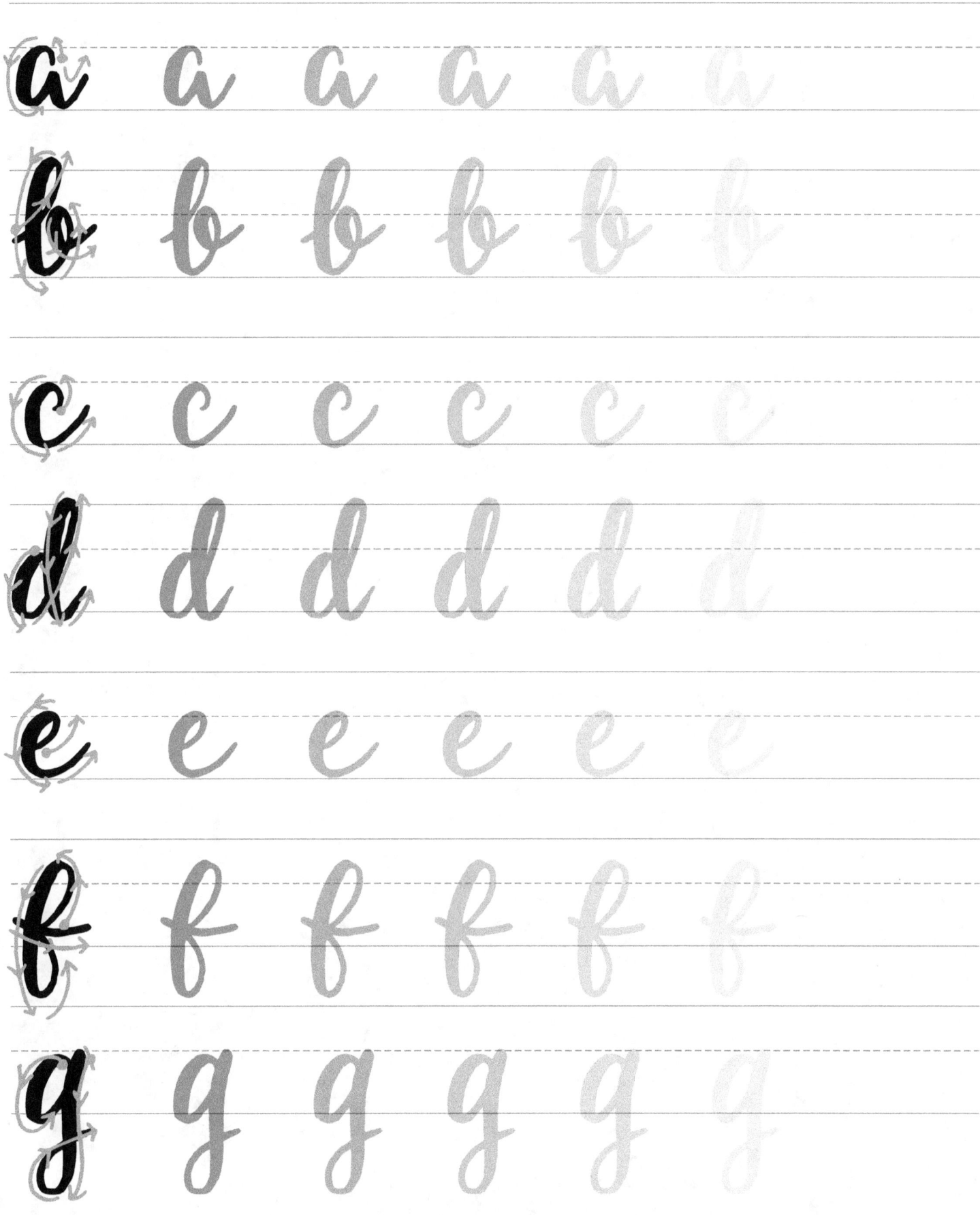

h h h h h h
i i i i i i
j j j j j j
k k k k k k
l l l l l l
m m m m m m
n n n n n n

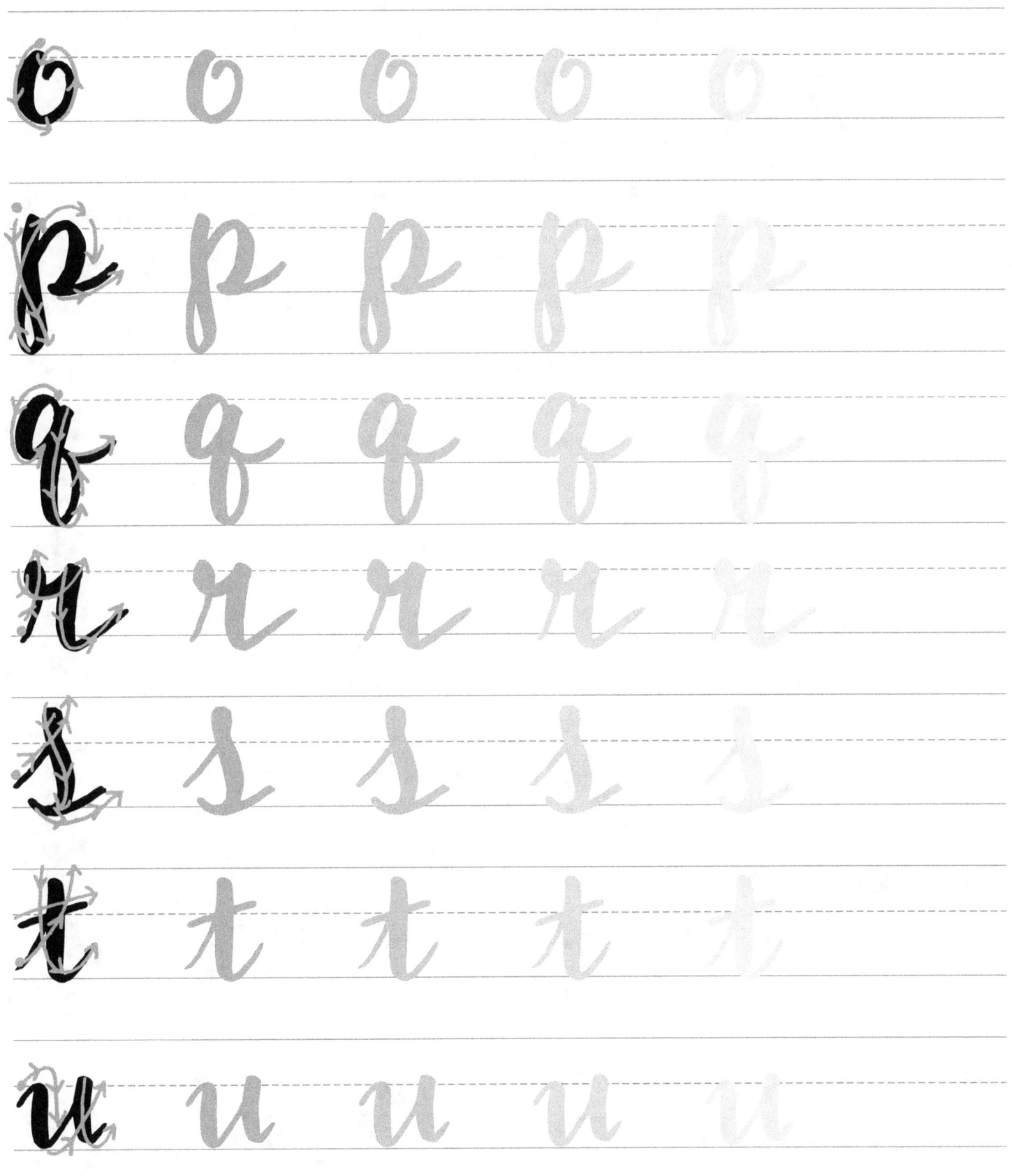

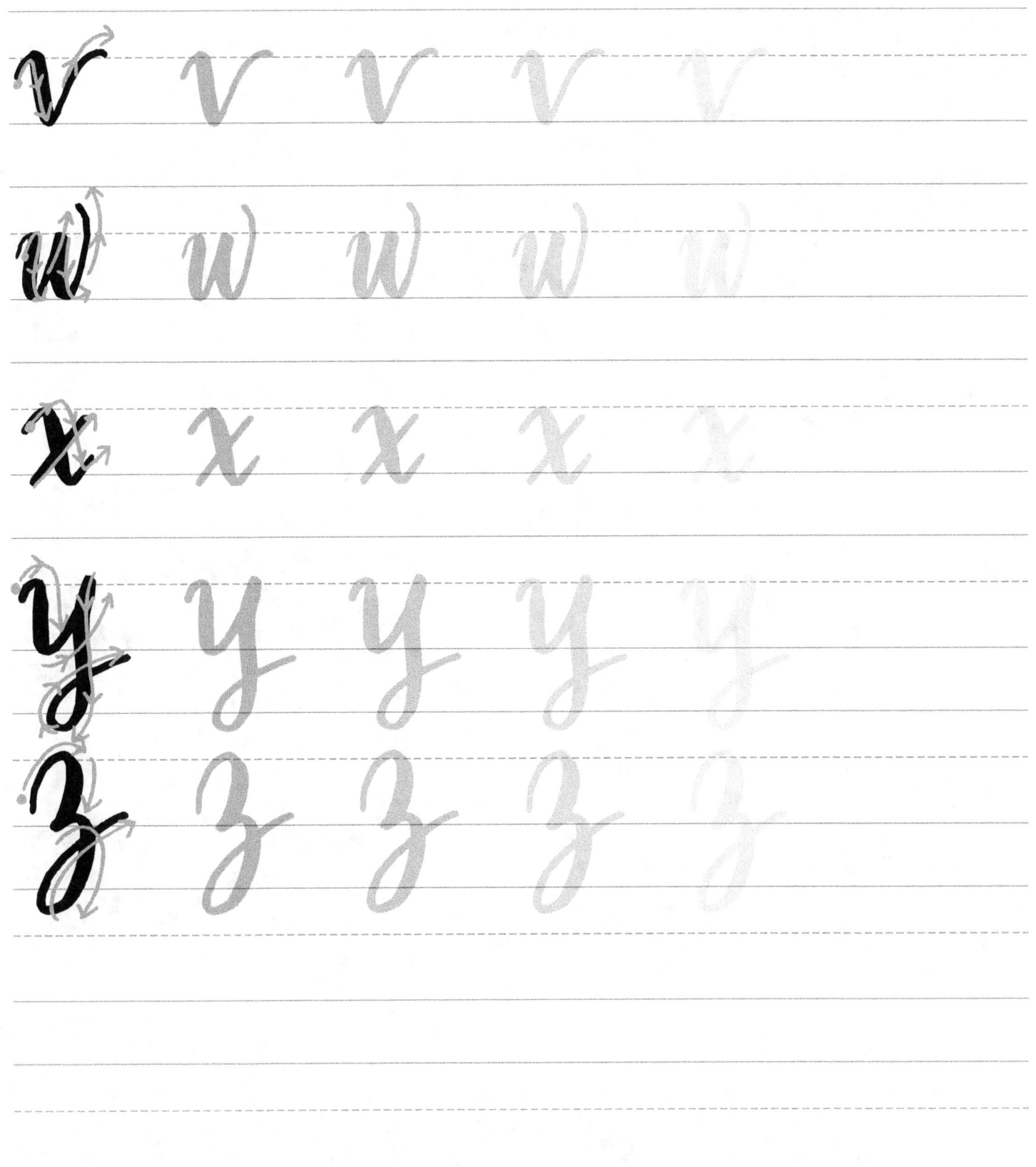

1 1 1 1 1 1 1
2 2 2 2 2 2 2
3 3 3 3 3 3 3
4 4 4 4 4 4 4
5 5 5 5 5 5 5
6 6 6 6 6 6 6
7 7 7 7 7 7 7

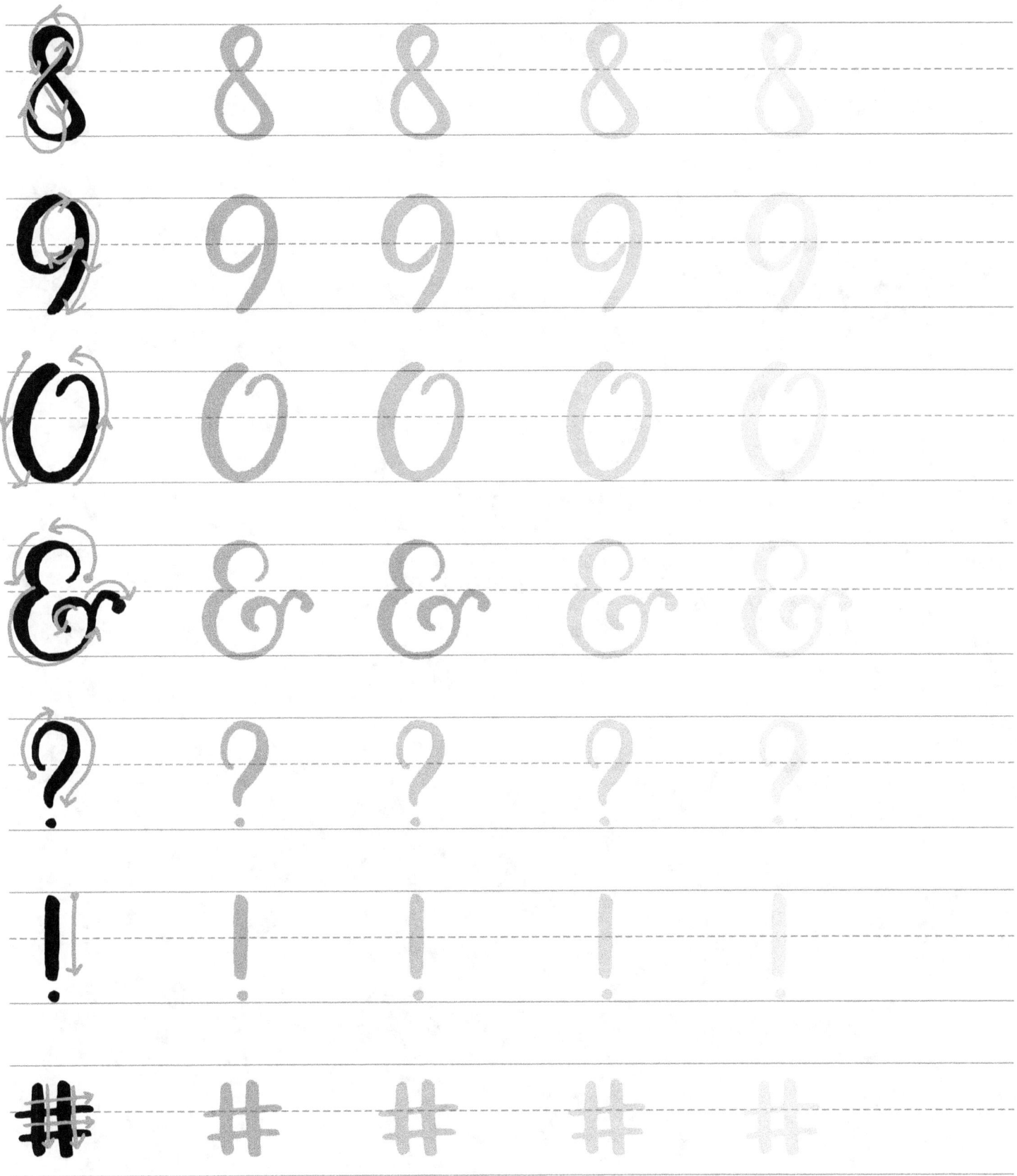

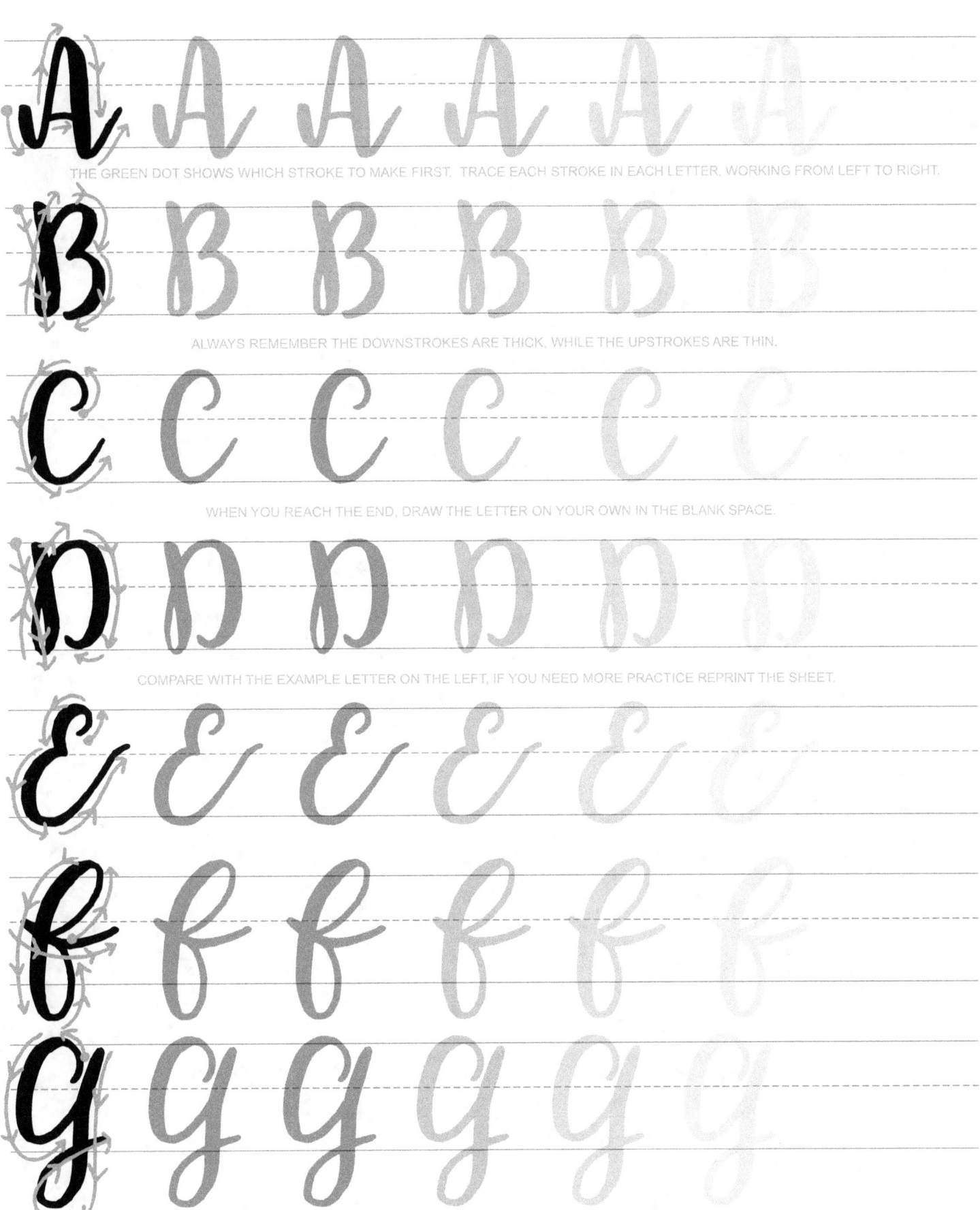

H H H H H
d d d d d
J J J J J
K K K K K
L L L L L
m m m m m m
n n n n n n

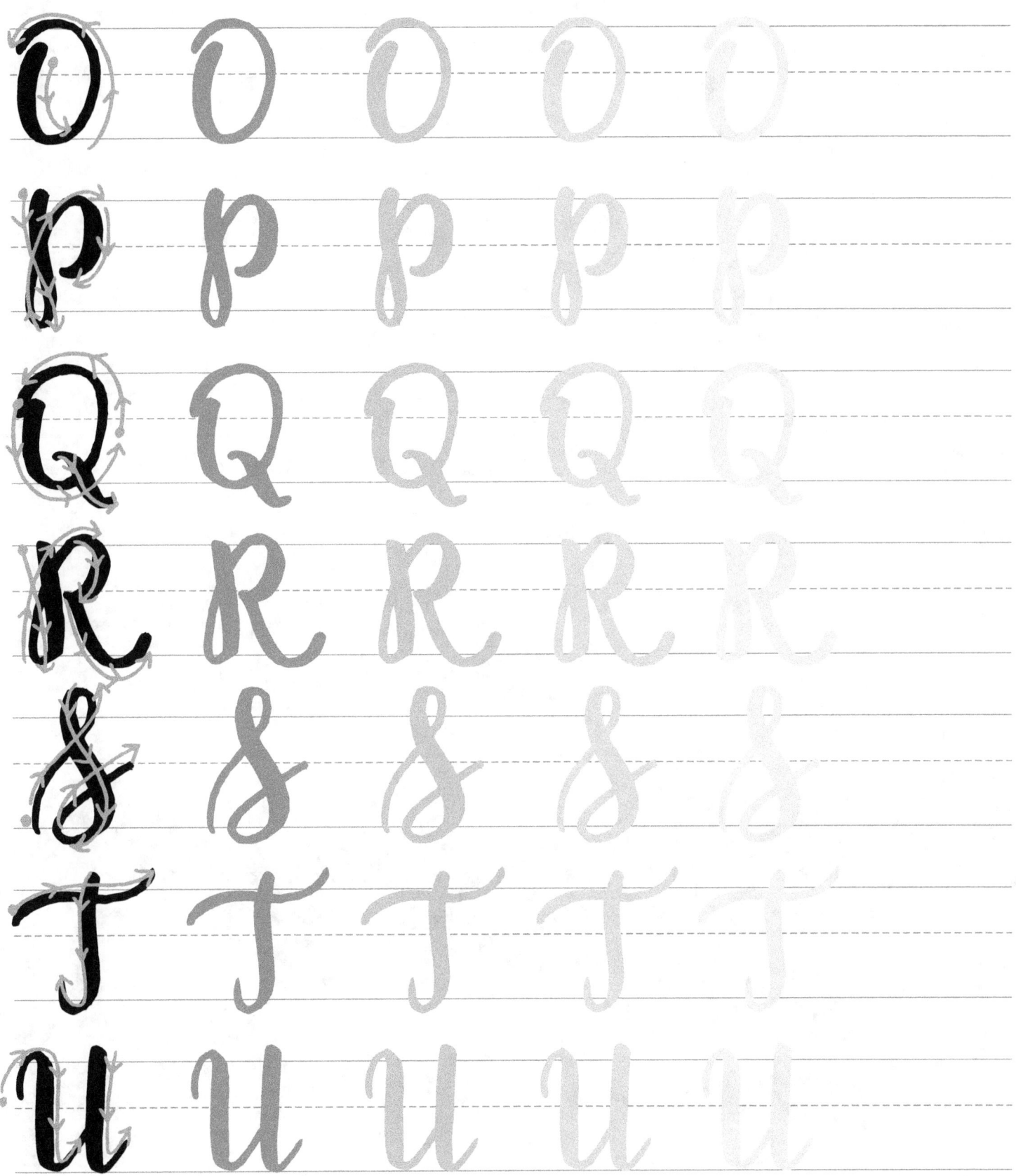

V V V V V V
W W W W W W
X X X X X X
Y Y Y Y Y Y
Z Z Z Z Z Z

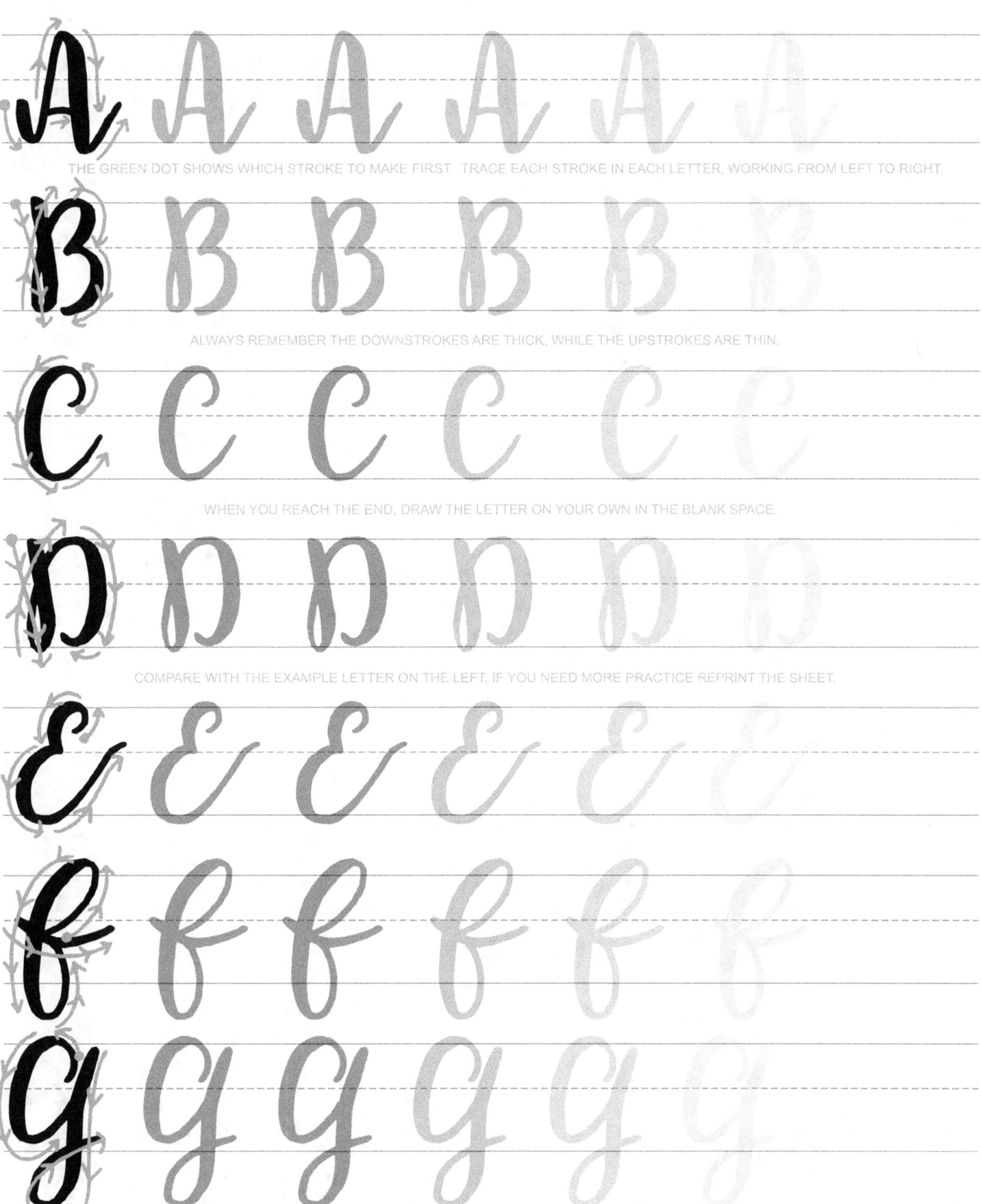

H H H H H

d d d d d

J J J J J

K K K K K

L L L L L

m m m m m

n n n n n

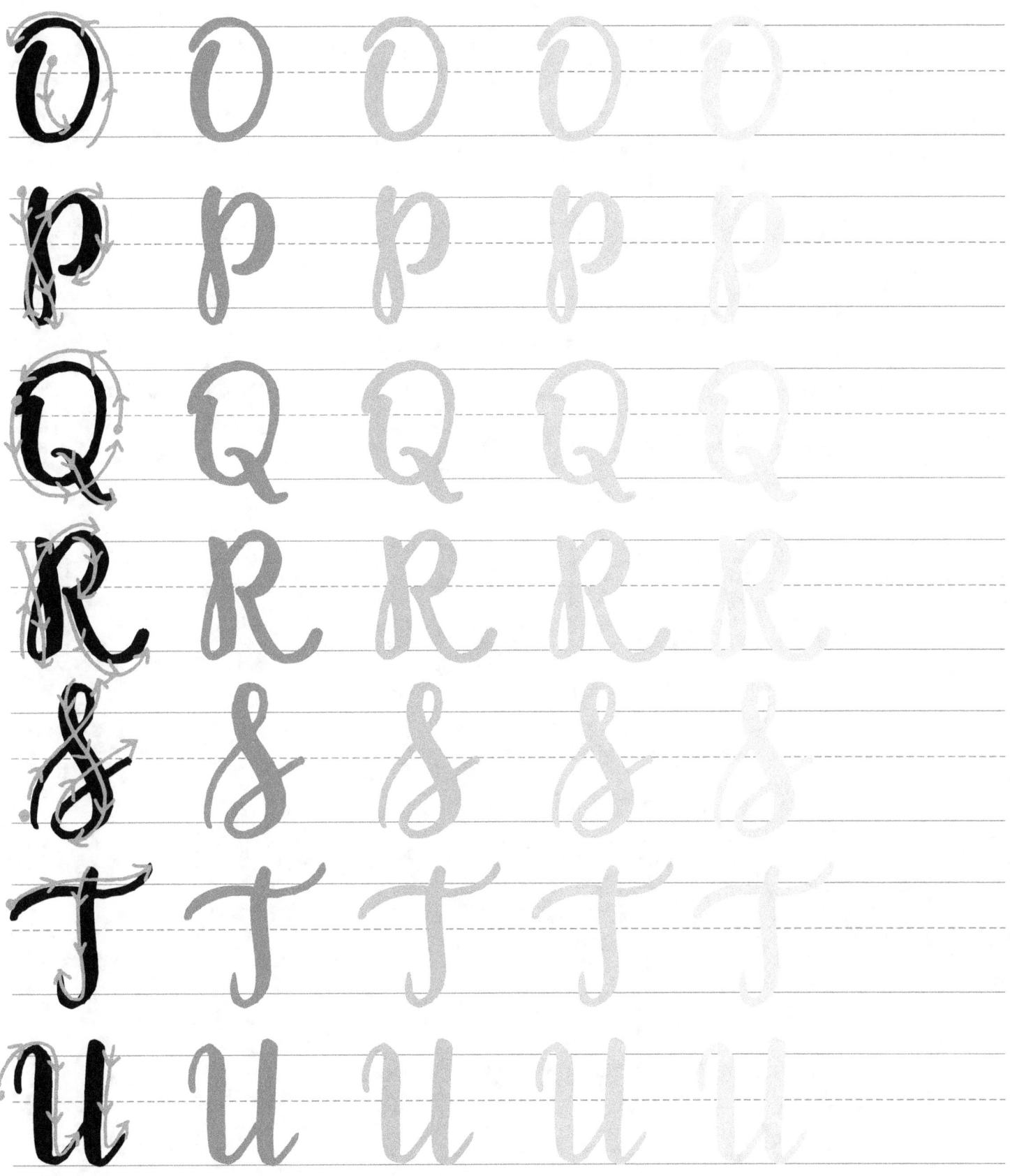

V V V V V
W W W W W
X X X X X
Y Y Y Y Y
Z Z Z Z Z

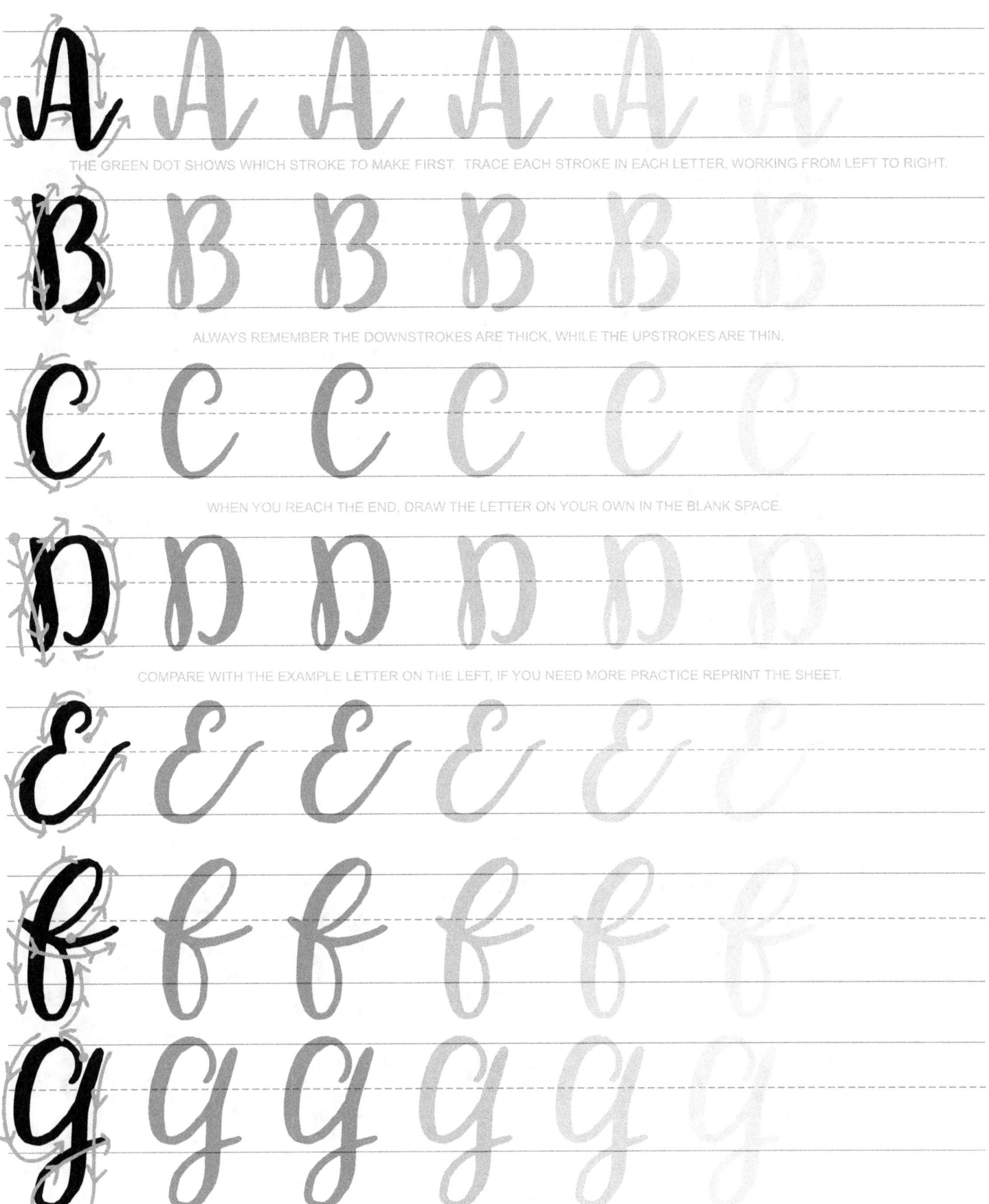

H H H H H

d d d d d

J J J J J

K K K K K

L L L L L

m m m m m

n n n n n

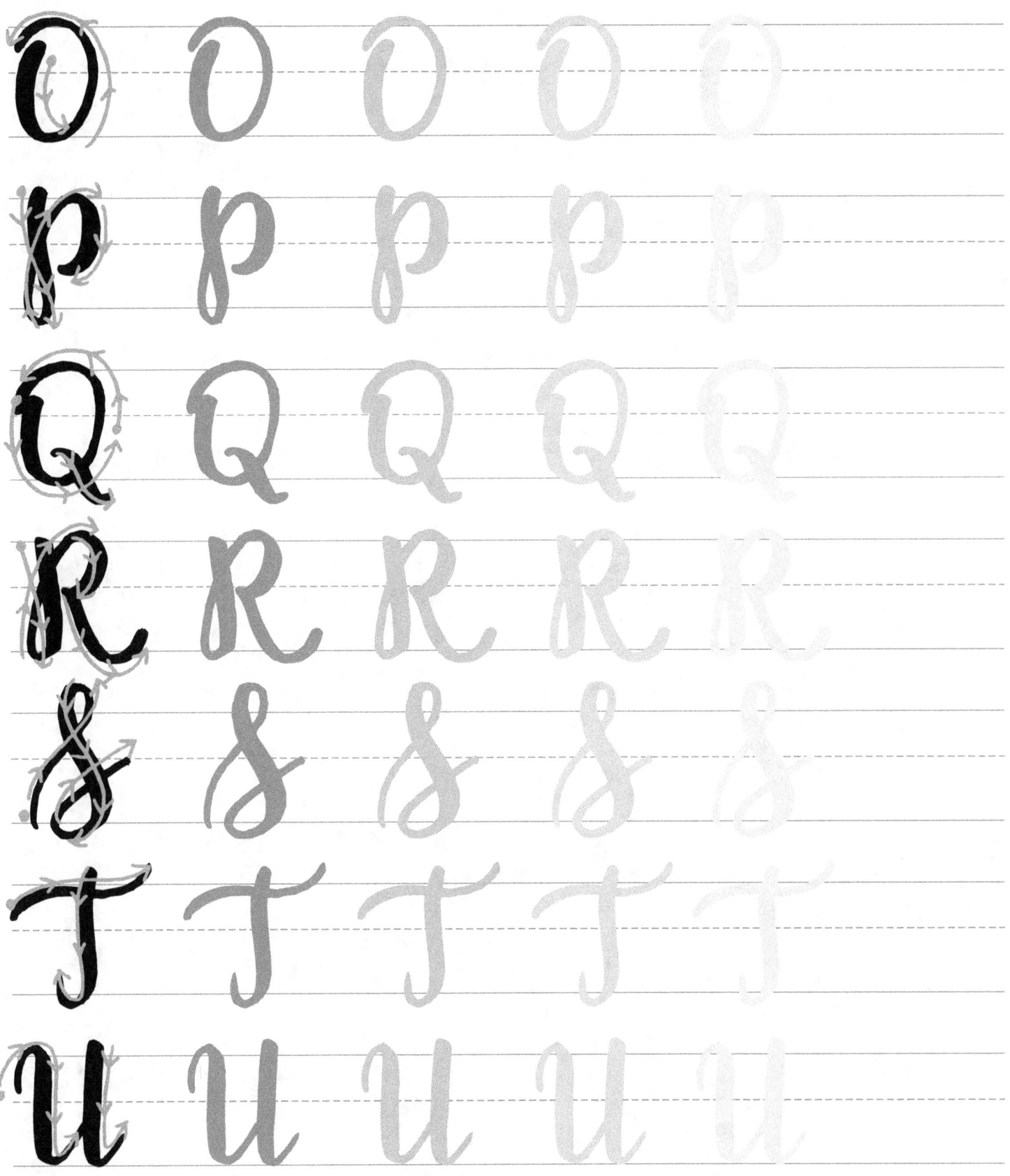

V V V V V
W W W W W
X X X X X
Y Y Y Y Y
Z Z Z Z Z

1 1 1 1 1 1 1

2 2 2 2 2 2 2

3 3 3 3 3 3 3

4 4 4 4 4 4 4

5 5 5 5 5 5 5

6 6 6 6 6 6 6

7 7 7 7 7 7 7

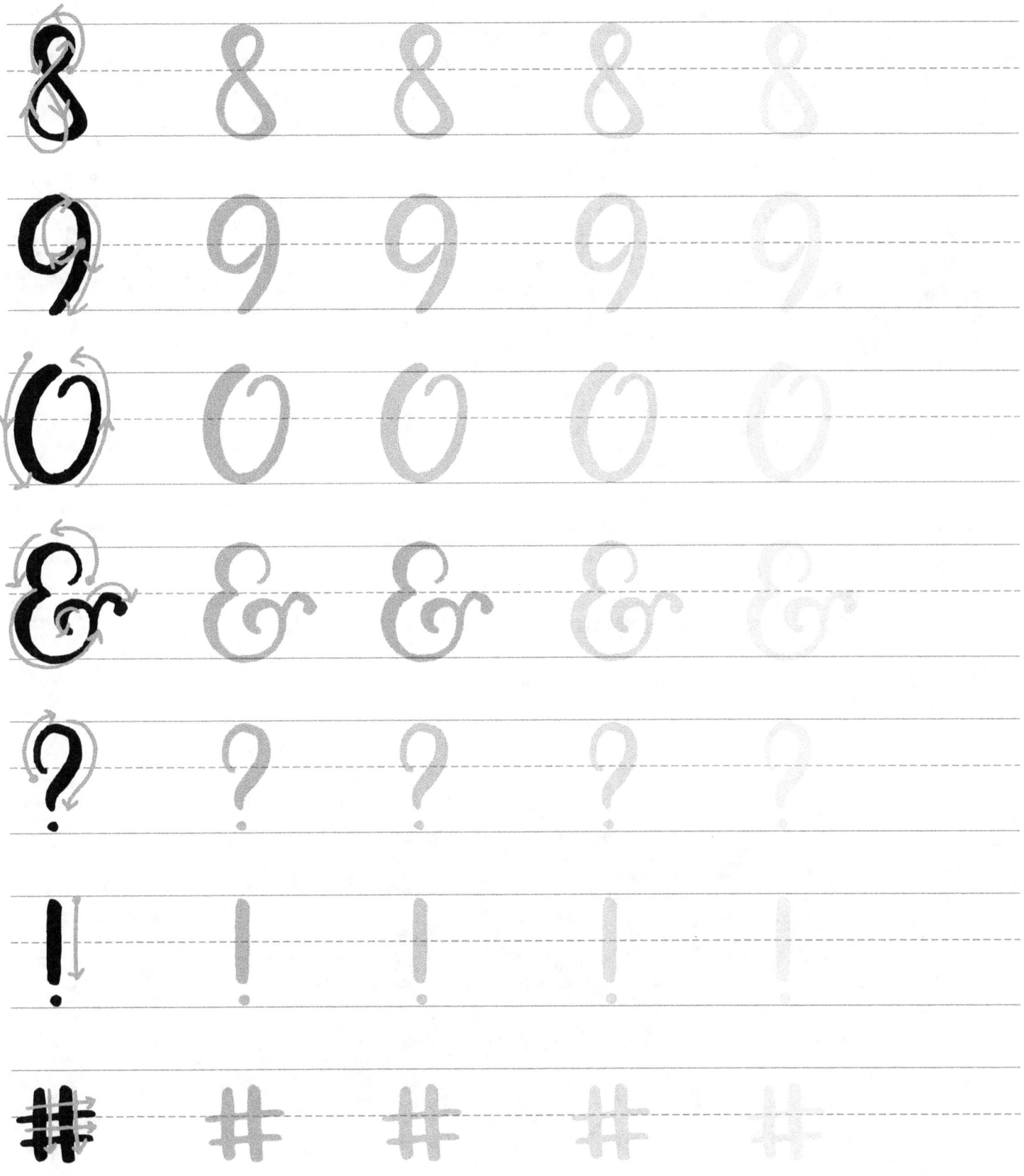

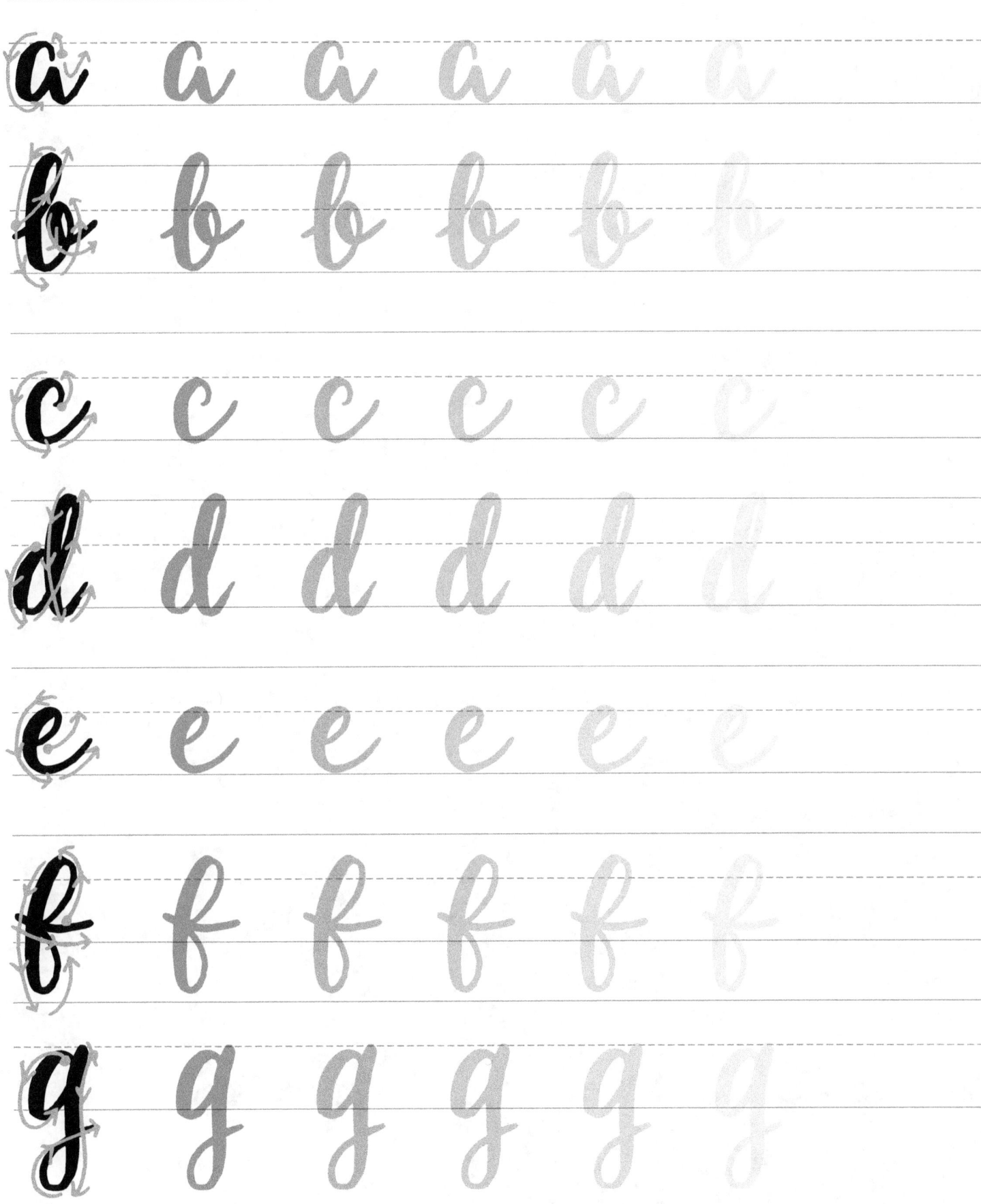

h h h h h
i i i i i
j j j j j
k k k k k
l l l l l
m m m m m
n n n n n

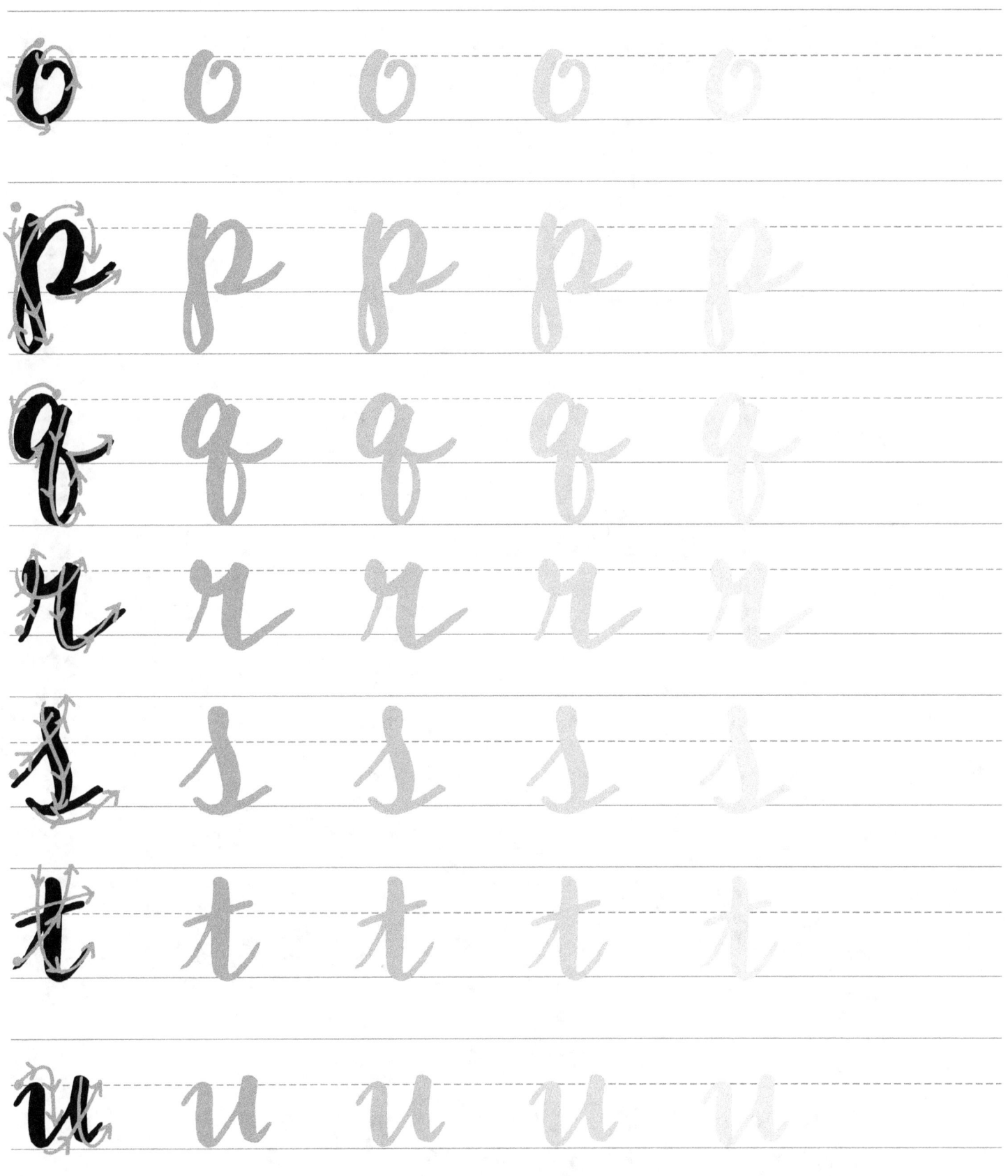

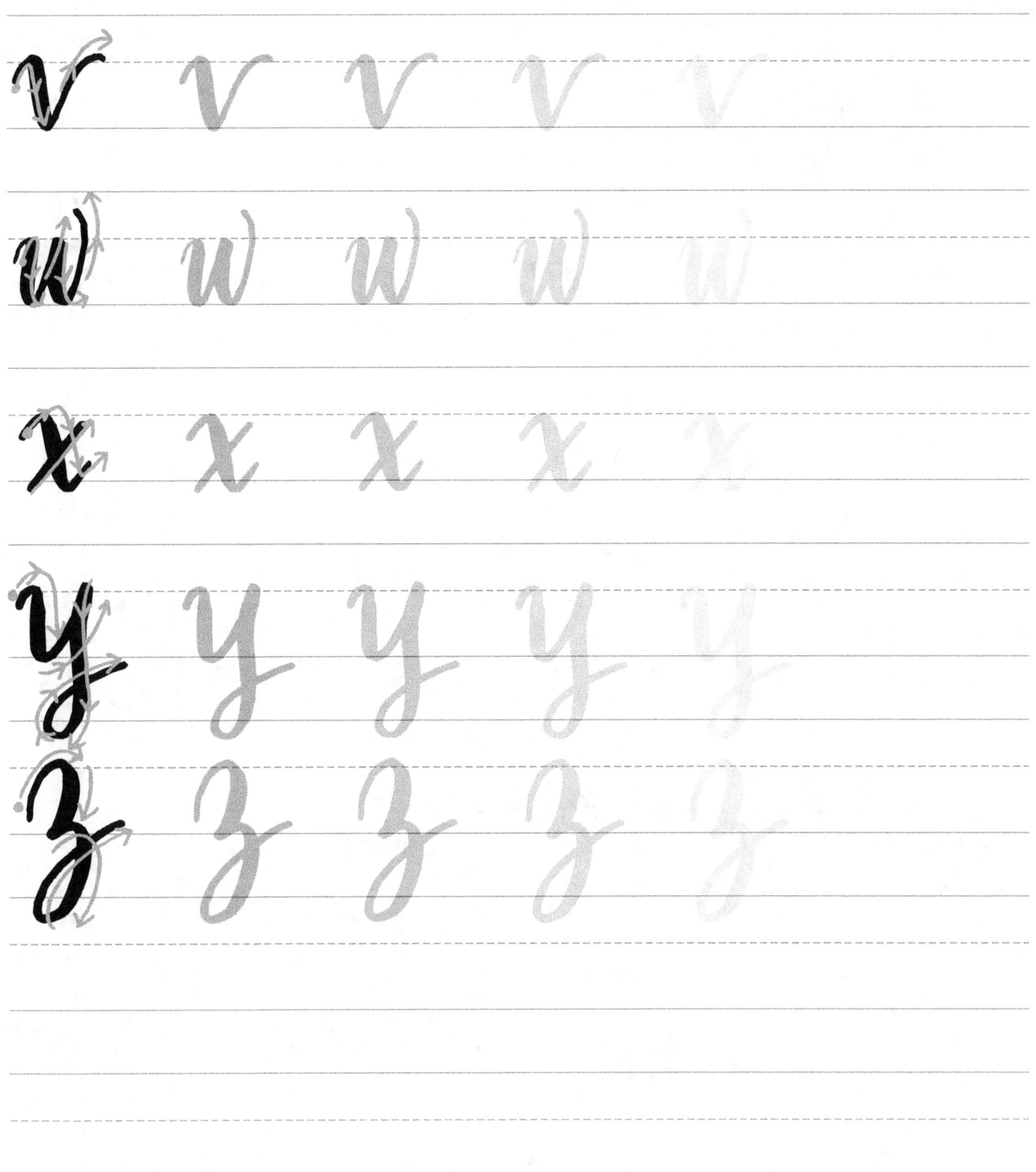

1 1 1 1 1 1 1

2 2 2 2 2 2 2

3 3 3 3 3 3 3

4 4 4 4 4 4 4

5 5 5 5 5 5 5

6 6 6 6 6 6 6

7 7 7 7 7 7 7

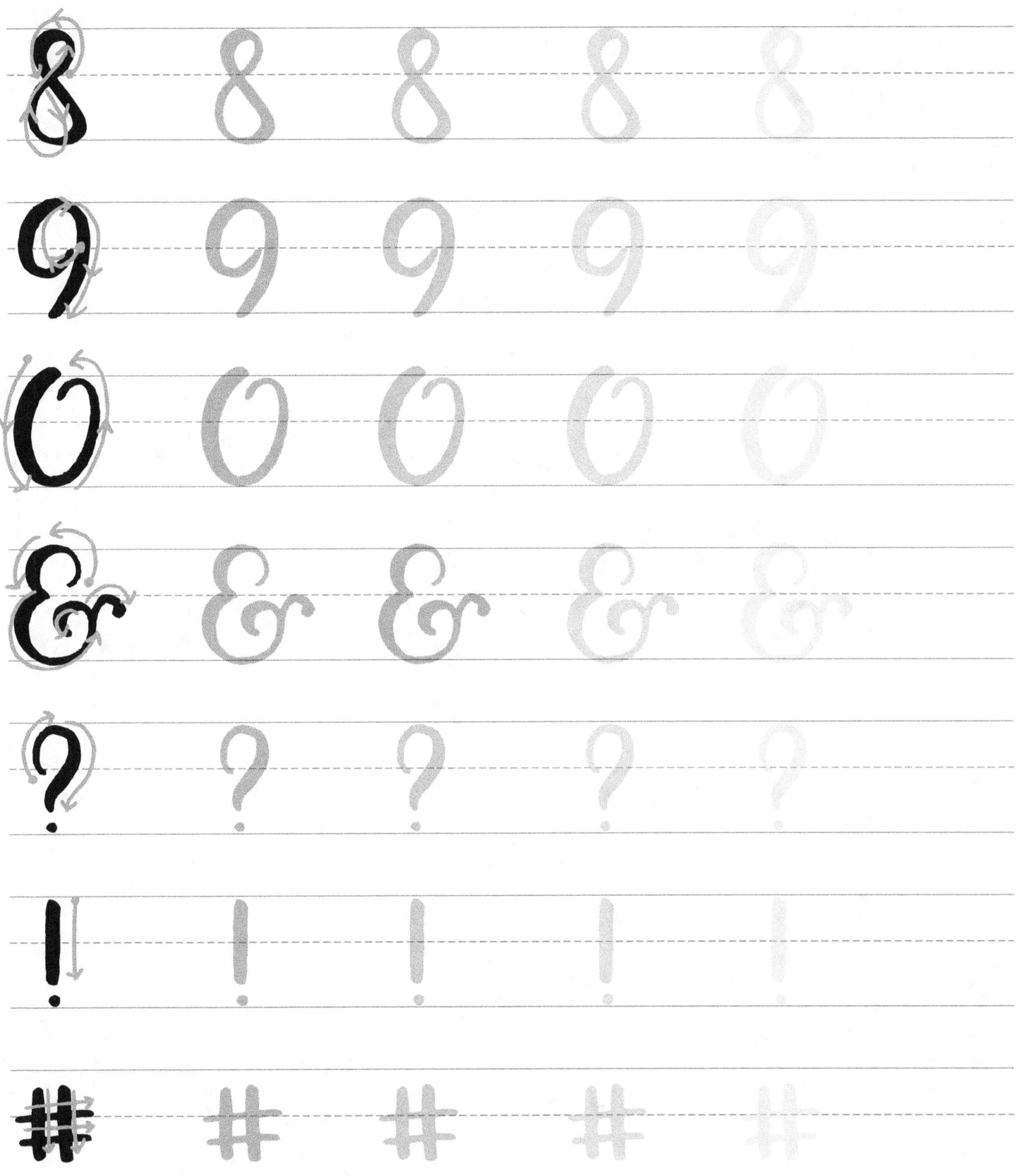

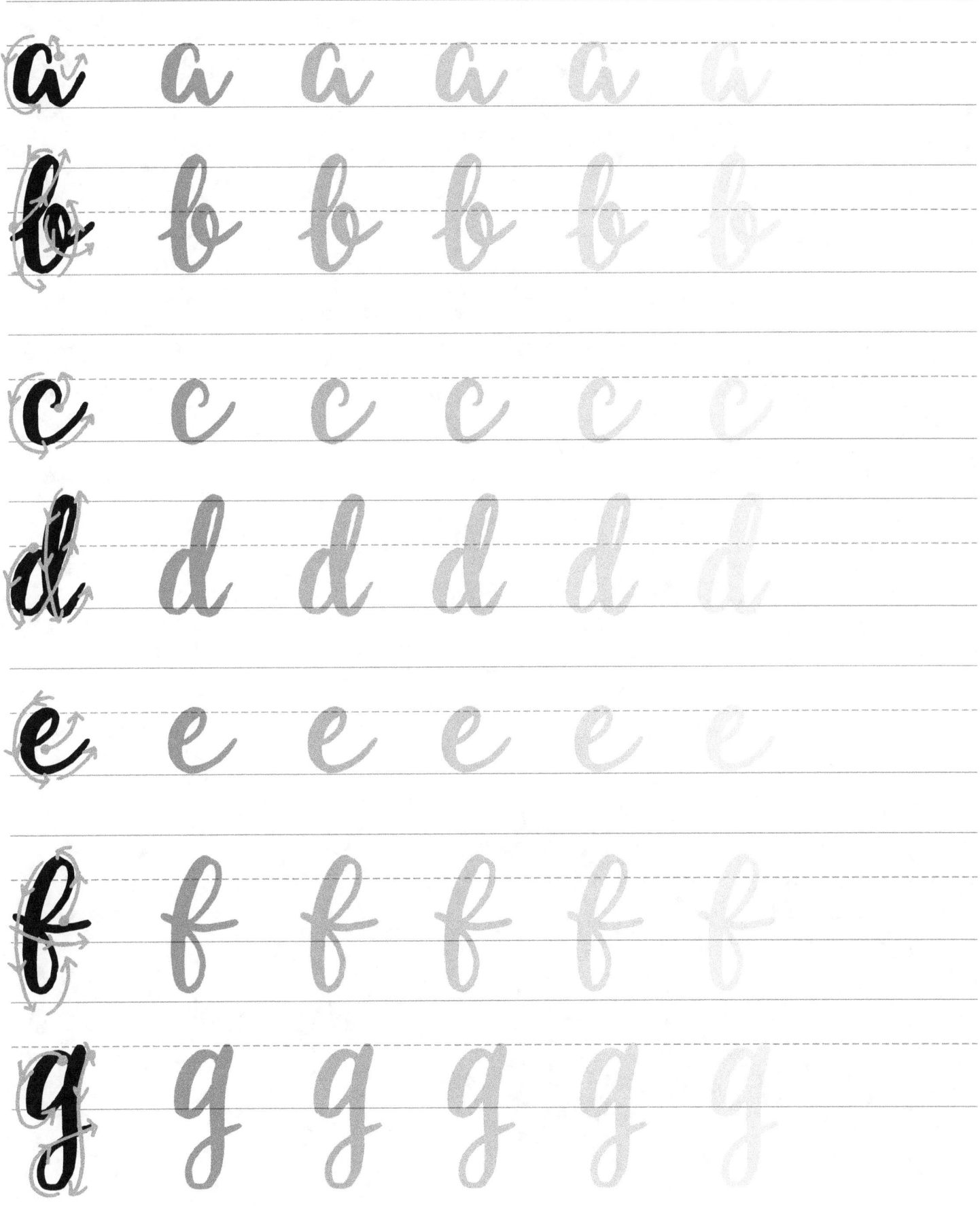

h h h h h h
i i i i i i
j j j j j j
k k k k k k
l l l l l l
m m m m m m
n n n n n n

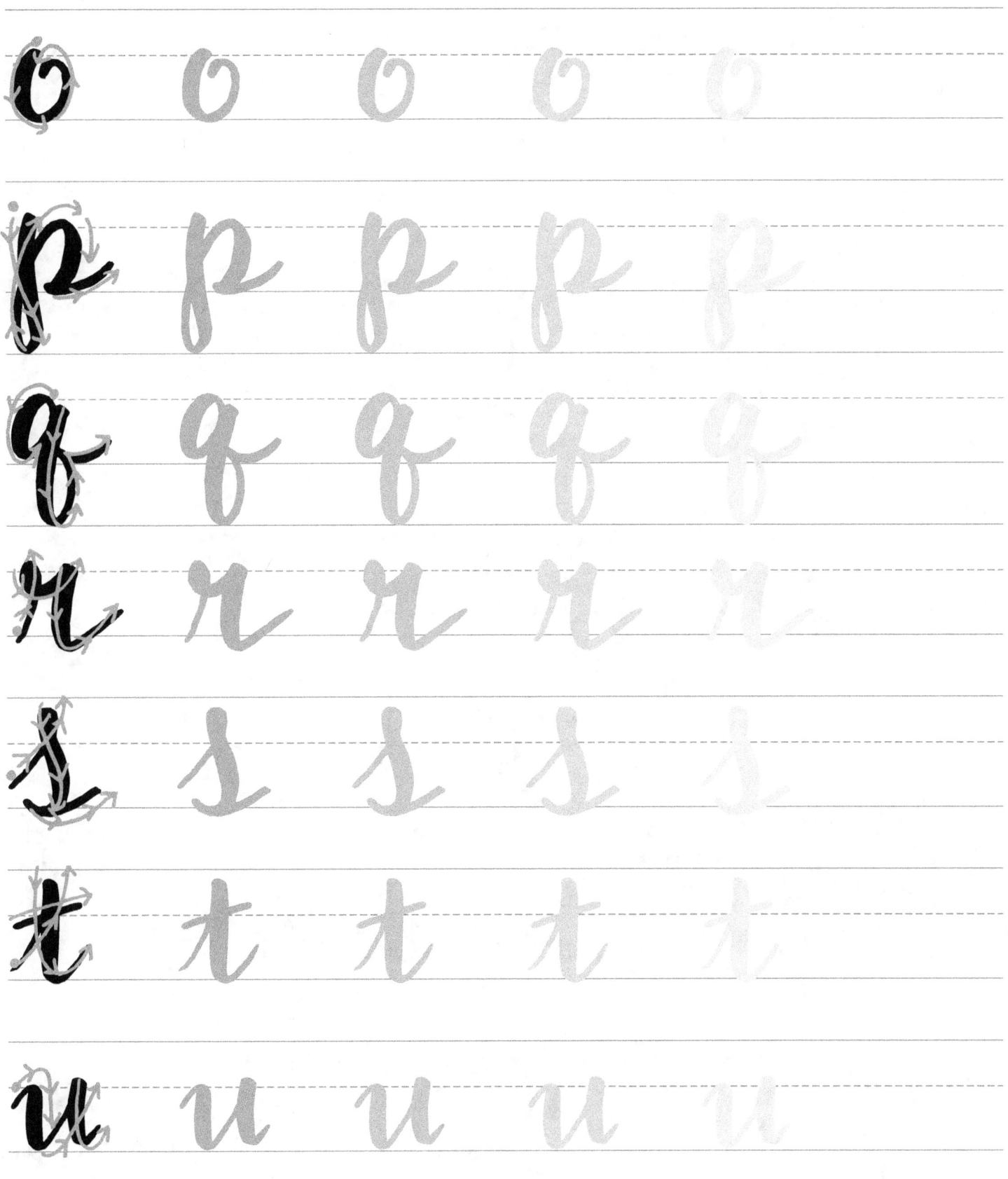

v v v v v
w w w w w
x x x x x
y y y y y
z z z z z

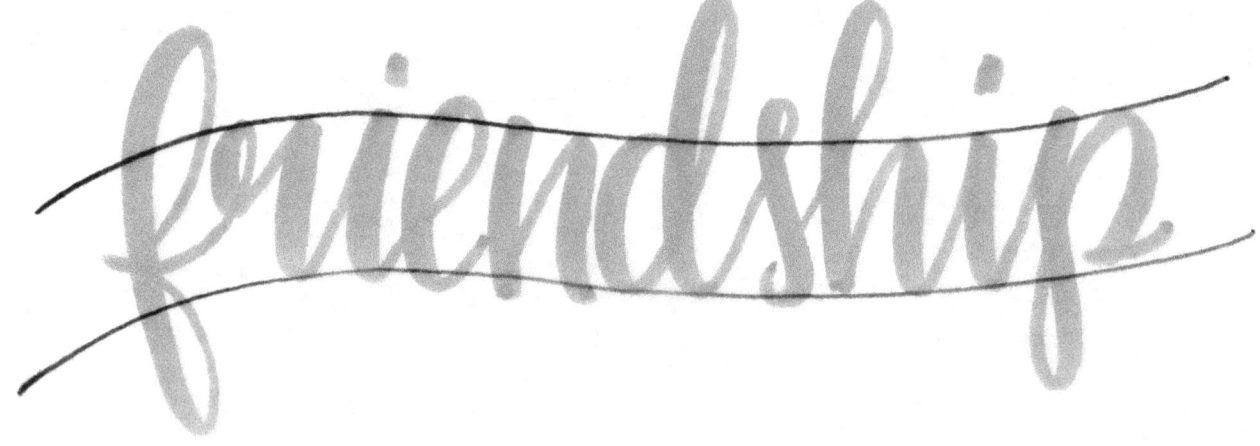

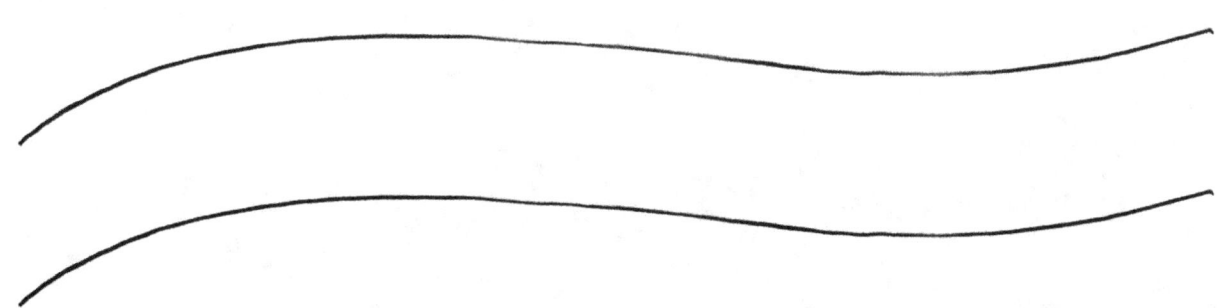

Here you will find a selection of lettered words. The finished word appears at the top. The middle layout shows the guidelines that were used to produce the lettering. At the bottom you will find empty guidelines to practice writing that word on your own. To start, trace over the middle example.

Varying the curve, angle or shape of the guidelines will give you different results. For a more free-form style use a zig-zag as your guideline, an example of which can be found in the next few pages.

Happiness

Happiness

friend

friend

Happy

Happy

Peace Love

Joy   Glee

freehand

freehand

Lettering

Lettering

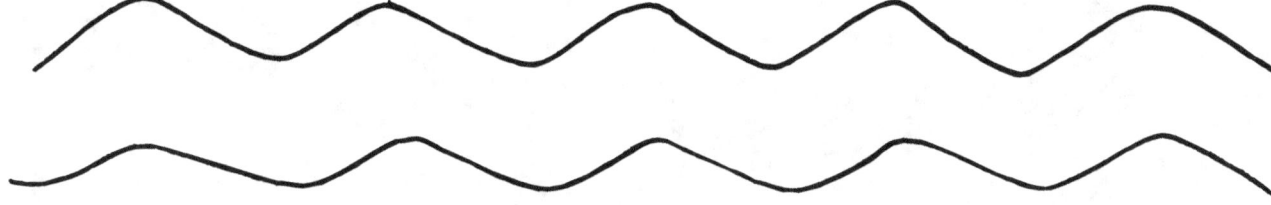

PRACTICING THESE STROKES WILL TRAIN YOU TO USE THE MARKER FOR THIN & THICK LETTER STROKES.

TRACE OVER EACH SHAPE IN SEQUENCE.

WHEN YOU REACH THE BLANK SPACE AT THE END, DRAW THE SHAPE ON YOUR OWN.

COMPARE YOUR FINAL SHAPE WITH THE REFERENCE SHAPE AT THE FAR LEFT.

PRACTICING THESE STROKES WILL TRAIN YOU TO USE THE MARKER FOR THIN & THICK LETTER STROKES.

TRACE OVER EACH SHAPE IN SEQUENCE.

WHEN YOU REACH THE BLANK SPACE AT THE END, DRAW THE SHAPE ON YOUR OWN.

COMPARE YOUR FINAL SHAPE WITH THE REFERENCE SHAPE AT THE FAR LEFT.

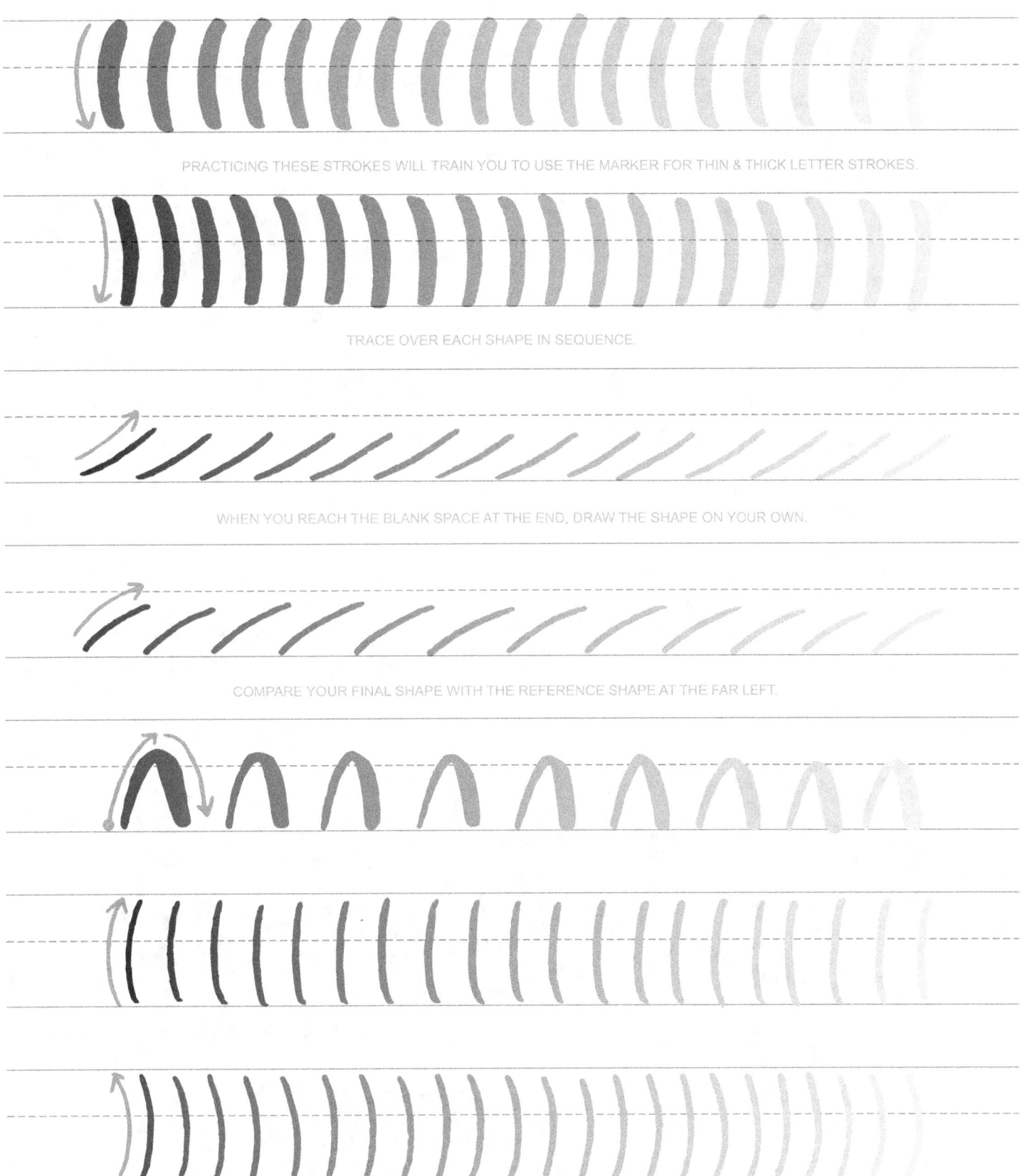

(C) 2017 CJ Hughes/ Easy Lettering Workbooks. All rights reserved. No sharing, resale or uploading permitted.

(C) 2017 CJ Hughes/ Easy Lettering Workbooks. All rights reserved. No sharing, resale or uploading permitted.

(C) 2017 CJ Hughes/ Easy Lettering Workbooks. All rights reserved. No sharing, resale or uploading permitted.

(C) 2017 CJ Hughes/ Easy Lettering Workbooks. All rights reserved. No sharing, resale or uploading permitted.

(C) 2017 CJ Hughes/ Easy Lettering Workbooks. All rights reserved. No sharing, resale or uploading permitted.

(C) 2017 CJ Hughes/ Easy Lettering Workbooks. All rights reserved. No sharing, resale or uploading permitted.

(C) 2017 CJ Hughes/ Easy Lettering Workbooks. All rights reserved. No sharing, resale or uploading permitted.

(C) 2017 CJ Hughes/ Easy Lettering Workbooks. All rights reserved. No sharing, resale or uploading permitted.

www.ingramcontent.com/pod-product-compliance
Lightning Source LLC
Chambersburg PA
CBHW080926220526
45465CB00008BA/2944